CONFESSIONS OF AN OVERCOMER:

THE TRUTH ABOUT THE WAIT

ROSZIEN KAY LEWIS

CONFESSIONS PUBLISHING

Confessions of An Overcomer: The Truth About the Wait
Copyright © 2017 by Roszien K. Lewis, Roszien Kay, LLC.
ISBN: 978-0-692-04587-9

Printed and bound in the United States of America.

Editor: Proofreadmybook.com
Cover Design and Cover Layout: Colbie Johnson
Photographer: Virgil Murray Photography

Confessions Publishing is a subsidiary of Roszien Kay LLC, Lancaster, CA 93536

For information regarding discounts on bulk purchase and all other inquiries, please contact us at roszien@gmail.com

CONTENTS

"Waiting on the manifestation of a promise is less about the promise and more about God preparing you for it."

FOREWORD

by Colbie Johnson

You would think that by now we would be accustom to waiting. We wait for almost everything. We wait in line to checkout at the store, in a drive-thru, and at amusement parks. Waiting has become an acceptable and expected part of life. So then why is it so hard to wait on God's promises, when we can wait in line for 5 hours, in the hot sun, for the newest iPhone? It's because we know what to expect. We can guess how much time it will take to wait in that drive-thru or choose the shortest line at Target to get out quicker. We can figure out the outcome and timetable in our day to day lives of things we must wait for.

However, we cannot figure out God's timing and how long we will actually have to wait, and that is the hardest part. The unknown and the constant wondering of when is this period going to end? When will the breakthrough happen? How much longer can I hold on?

The truth about the wait is you will always be waiting for some manifestation of a promise if you are walking in the will of God. We go from glory to glory, from faith to faith, and victory to victory. After you attain one promise, the Father reveals another level for you, another promise to wait for.

The truth is the wait may be ugly, tiring, and at times frustrating. The truth is the wait is not something that can be bypassed. This book will help you to understand what God wants to do in you through the process, as well as what God wants you to do.

INTRODUCTION

Living in a world where you can have everything at almost an instant has made waiting for anything unpopular and sometimes unheard of. People jump in and out of relationships without batting an eye. Employers fire and hire employees at rapid speeds. Employees start a job one week, quit that same job by the next week, and interview for another job later that day.

Our current culture has made waiting unattractive. Anytime someone says they're waiting to get into a relationship with the right person, waiting for a job, or the optimal time to do something, people look at them as if something is wrong with them. Society assumes anyone waiting for love is doing so because there is some deficiency in that person. Or that anyone waiting for the right job or time to step out in faith is actually lazy. Though these assumptions may be true in some instances, they neglect to consider the importance and actual reasoning behind the choice to wait.

This book will take you on a journey through my wait season. After making all the decisions for my own life, I decided to completely surrender my will to God and allow Him to guide my every move. This decision required me to consult and wait on God concerning my career, whether I would date, who I would marry, what friendships I would form, and much more.

As I waited, I ultimately learned waiting on God was less about obtaining promises. Instead, the wait was mostly about God shaping and molding me into the woman He created me to be. Fasten your seat belt as I take you on a ride that spills the beans on the good, the bad, and ugly side of waiting the kingdom way.

WHAT IS THE WAIT?

The dictionary definition for waiting is "to stay in a place until an expected event happens, until someone arrives, until it is your turn to do something, etc." When I encountered this definition, I imagined standing in a line at the grocery store or my favorite department store. I thought about the many emotions one may feel while waiting. For example, if the wait is short and swift, a feeling of relief and calmness touches the soul. If the wait is a little longer than expected, impatience sets in but quickly disappear when the wait ends. But when the wait is long, a host of emotions are felt causing the person to become agitated, annoyed, or disgruntled. Regardless of which scenario you may experience, waiting affects you in a way.

When I surrendered my will completely to Christ, I wasn't prepared for my journey of waiting. By that time, I had heard stories about someone waiting for a mate or even a job opportunity. It seemed as if everything happened quickly for them. Naively, I assumed my waiting period would be similar to theirs. Prior to waiting, I had always received things in the time period I had planned. I had no other reason to assume things would be any different as I waited for God's timing. However, while waiting, I quickly realized this was not the case. After I surrendered my will to God, my plans became irrelevant. Instantly, my time frame didn't mean anything and was irrelevant because it had been according to the world's timeframe. Once I said yes to the Lord's will, my waiting period had become according to the King's timetable.

I've discovered through trial and error there is a distinct difference between kingdom waiting and waiting according to the world's time clock. The world tells us we can make things happen when we want, how we want, and with whom we want it to happen with. The world says "you want it now, all you have to do is work harder, and it will happen quicker."

When you're waiting according to the King's timetable, there is a tremendous difference. One of the first and most profound difference is that you have no control. Unlike with waiting by the world's timeframe, working harder will not get you anything or anywhere sooner than the appointed time. Another difference is you cannot make things happen when, with whom, and how you want them to happen. Things happen according to the will and timing of God!

Initially, I did not understand or didn't want to comprehend waiting according to the King's timetable. I wanted what I wanted, and that was it. When I didn't get what I wanted, I unsuccessfully tried to manipulate God. I would tell Him, "Okay, I'm going to do what you said, but I'm going to need you to do this and that." I would even quote scriptures like *"Ask, and it will be given to you;"* (Matthew 7:7) to assist with the manipulation. I even went as far as praying for a job opportunity or relationship to manifest using these flawed tactics.

No matter how often I attempted to manipulate God with my flawed tactics, God did not budge. No matter how much I prayed, how many kingdom assignments I fulfilled, or how many scriptures I quoted, the King did not move. This caused instant frustration. I had crying fits. I had brief moments of rage. I even became upset when the Holy Spirit rebuked me for my actions.

When my fits and tantrums did not work, I became desperate. During my desperate moments, I told God I wasn't going to keep living for Him. I told Him I wasn't going to wait for Him to move; I would proceed without Him. (Even though I knew this was far from the truth).

This cycle repeated itself until I finally realized God was not moved by my threats. I came to admit that I had made the conscious decision to tell Him I would surrender my will to Him. As a result, I finally realized that meant that I had to give up all control. With this realization, I finally accepted God would not allow a door to open if it were not His will. God would not let me leave a place before my assignment was done. And God would not permit me to date just anyone or take just any job because He had control.

Once I realized God was the one in control, I was faced with the realization that I had prolonged my season of waiting. The time I spent trying to convince God my timeframe was better or more important than His, resulted in me not moving forward. It caused me to experience moments where I felt as though I was standing still while everyone around me was passing me by. I felt as though I was at a subway station or bus stop just standing there as passengers hurried along. They hastened along as I stood still watching. No matter how much I tried to move along with them, I still stood still. And it was all because I spent so much time trying to manipulate God.

After facing this reality, I decided I would commit to God's timing more than before. As a result; over time, I developed the capacity to accept and tolerate God's timing. I no longer threw tantrums because of delays. I grew to understand that kingdom waiting included moments of "delay." This was not an easy process. It required me to develop more patience. It needed me to pray for strength when I felt weary. It demanded I recite scripture like Habakkuk 2:2-3 *"And the Lord answered me: 'Write the vision; make it plain on tablets, so he may run who reads it. 3 For still the vision awaits its appointed time; it hastens to the end- it will not lie. If it seems slow, wait for it; it will surely come; it will not delay,"* over and over again until they took root in my heart. The more I repeated these steps, the stronger I became as I waited according to the King's timing.

WHY WAIT?

Isaiah 55:8 (KJV)~For my thoughts are not your thoughts, neither are your ways my ways, saith the LORD.

Even though I wanted to believe I had everything figured out, I didn't. Even though I had these grand plans for my life, they weren't bigger than God's plans for me. Once I realized I had no other choice but to wait on God, I stopped driving myself as crazy as I had been. God's plans were far greater than mine.

The main reason the Lord's plans are better is because He knows everything. What I found as I looked at my reflection was that I knew nothing. I had no idea what the next hour would bring let along the next day, year, or month. I came to realize the reason I had to wait was because the Lord knew the path I should take. He knew what road would bring me destruction. He knew what way would bring me life. The Lord even knew the numbers of hairs on my head. And He knew the moment my eyes would open and close.

Aside from knowing when things would occur, the Lord knows the heart of men. Upon meeting a potential mate, friend, or employer, we only see the outer appearance. We are only privy to know what they expose to us. We aren't able to understand their secret motives. We can't see their impure desires. We can't perceive beyond the outer shell no matter how hard we try. Though we aren't able to behold beyond what's in front of us, God can. He is the only one with the ability to protect us. He knows when a person's heart is incapable of being loving and gentle. The Lord sees when a person's heart is even incapable of receiving love. Because of this, waiting on the Lord is necessary.

Failure to wait for the Lord's timing can result in many failures. Stepping out too soon may result in us being ill-equipped. Failure to wait may result in our character, morals, or ethics not being fully developed. Even worse, our inability to wait may result in the incapability to see or walk in our God-given purpose.

When we move ahead of God's divine timing, we experience abortion of dreams, visions, and godly connections. The process of waiting can easily be compared to the birth process of a fetus. Waiting delays a premature death. When a baby is born too early, there is an increased risk of death. Though there are lungs in the chest cavity, the premature baby's breathing may be compromised. The lack of oxygen to the baby's brain may very well result in the baby's inability to move. If born too soon, the baby's eyelids won't be fully developed to open. And even worse, the baby's limbs could be severely affected to the point of deformity.

As long as the baby remained in the womb according to the proper TIME, it continued to be protected as it developed. The baby receives the correct amount of nutrients. The baby's lungs, limbs, eyes, and other vital organs go through the process of development. As a result, the baby's survival rate increases as it approaches its proper time for delivery.

As we remain in the womb of God's timing, we are more than likely to be who He intends for us to be. The areas where we are underdeveloped will become fully developed. The areas that need to be uprooted and cut off will be removed. Whatever is needed will only occur by allowing God to work on us as we wait for the manifestation of His promises.

DEVELOPING TRUST

Proverbs 3:5~ Trust in the Lord with all your heart and lean not on your own understanding.

Trust is the "belief that someone or something is reliable, good, honest, effective, etc."

During my process of waiting for the manifestation of the promises God had promised me, I was forced to face the reality that I hadn't truly trusted anyone, including God. At that time, I honestly didn't know how to trust.

My past had taught me to trust no one and keep a question mark over everyone's head. This even went for family. I built high, thick walls around my heart and mind once I realized I couldn't trust my parents. My mother failed to protect me from the man who molested me from the age of 11-14. My father consistently lied to me as he went in and out of my life. As a result, over time, I decided everyone I came in contact with would betray me in one way or another; therefore, trust was unnecessary.

I carried this flawed notion into my relationship with God. Because of this, God took His time with showing me I could trust Him. The process was very slow and careful. I was put into many situations where I only had God to rely on. And with each situation, I came closer and closer to trusting God. He had always been consistent as long as I walked within His will for my life. He never left me. When I had nothing, He sent people to provide for me. When I was lonely, He was my comfort and much more. Because He never let me down, I gained the ability to trust Him with all my heart.

LEARNING SUBMISSION

Psalm 143:10 (KJV)~Teach me to do thy will; for thou art my God: thy spirit is good; lead me into the land of uprightness.

Submission is "the state of being obedient: the act of accepting the authority or control of someone else." Hearing the word submission made me cringe, made my skin crawl, and my blood boil. The very idea of allowing anyone to lead or guide me was completely out of the question. I refused to allow anyone to have "control" over me or anything connected to me.

My negative feelings towards submission were the product of my childhood. Those whom I submitted to completely shattered my trust. As a result, I promised myself when I became an adult; I would never put myself in the position where others had any kind of control over me.

After learning to trust God, I decided to break my promise to myself; I started to submit to God. The more I worked on submitting to God, the more I was able to see the areas which really needed work. I was able to identify the areas where I had no problem submitting to Him because there was no feeling of vulnerability. For example, I had no problem refusing to drink when God told me not to. I had no issue or struggle with not cursing. However, the Lord had to do a major work on me when it came to submitting to His will with relationships and fornication. I knew 1 Corinthians 6:19-20(NIV) stated: *"Do you not know that your bodies are temples of the Holy Spirit, who is in you, whom you have received from God? You are not your own; you were bought at a price. Therefore honor God with your bodies."* But I had issues with submitting that area of my life because the dysfunctional relationship I had been in brought me some sense of security. It made me feel "loved." At the time, it offered me the intimacy I had not yet tapped into with God.

When God told me to cut the relationship off, I refused to submit to His will. There I was, wanting to experience the fullness of

God but didn't want to follow His instructions. I fought against submitting that relationship to God for a couple of years. I had my mind made up; I would partially submit to God's will, and that was that.

Unfortunately for me, things in my life got worse. I was constantly afraid of God turning me over to my reprobate mind because I willfully disobeyed Him. During this time, I went to church every time the door opened, worshipped Him from a broken place, read His word, all while continuing to be yoked with someone God told me to leave. I wanted to do what I wanted to do, how I wanted to do it, and still serve God in the process.

My lukewarm lifestyle came to a sudden halt. God had been showing me dreams in which my then fiancé had been cheating. I could even hear the Lord telling me to leave him. I argued with God at every turn because I didn't want to submit that. In an attempt to convince the Lord to change His mind, I told Him how afraid I was. In return, God said He would take care of me. I explained to God I couldn't provide for two small children on my own. The Lord said that He was my provider. I informed God it would hurt too much. The Lord instead said He would take care of my heart. No matter what the Lord told me, I refused to submit that area of my life to Him.

My refusal to submit to God continued until God closed doors. I had been trying to find a job to take care of my children. It seemed no matter how much I met the job's qualifications; I didn't receive a return call. I prayed so much for a door to open only to have them remain shut. The entire time, God kept saying: "Leave him." I kept refusing to submit. Doors continued to stay closed. I refused to listen to the Lord until I had no other choice. One day, while in church, my Pastor stopped his sermon to say "I don't know who this is for but God said He ain't gonna open another door to bless you to bless him." I sat there broken. I felt as though a knife had been logged in my heart. I felt like someone had turned that knife as he spoke. I knew God had been speaking directly to me. I knew what I had to do.

I couldn't live with the fact that if I didn't submit to God in every area of my life, doors would remain closed. I needed God's favor. I needed certain doors to open so that I would be able to care for my daughters. A few days after hearing God's last warning, I decided it was time. I ended the engagement.

After ending the engagement, I wasn't prepared for what I would experience. God, unlike those in my life, had kept His promise again. My heart never felt pain. I didn't shed one tear from the breakup. Less than two weeks after the breakup, a door finally opened; I found a job. From that moment onward, I continued to take small steps towards submitting to God and His will for my life.

The process of submission was not an easy process. However, over time, it became easier. The further I sat before God's word; I entered into more submission. The more I digested, read and processed, submitting to God's word became even easier. The more I prayed, listened to, and followed God's instruction, the more natural submission became. Even when, on rare occasions, I would go against what God said, it was easy for me to get back on course because I knew submitting to Him was what was best for my life.

HEARING GOD'S VOICE

John 10:27 (NIV)~My sheep listen to my voice; I know them, and they follow me.

During the wait, I became familiar with the voice of God. Before my decision to wait on God, I was yoked up with people. I either had people around hanging out and partying. Or I was either laid up in the bed with a man or on a date with one. I didn't have time for God. At that time, I didn't know how to hear God's voice let alone obey it. My life was filled with the chaos and cares of this world.

Once I submitted every aspect of myself to God, I became familiar with His voice. For some people, they hear God's voice in the same manner they hear the voice of people. For me, this was not the case. God's voice has always been still. It has always brought peace and comfort. It has always been loving. Sometimes, I hear it as the wind blows. Sometimes, I hear it through a song. Other times, it is through complete silence. At times, I hear it through another person's heartbeat. On some occasions, I hear it through a surge of thoughts or visions. It can also come in the dead of night. No matter what form God's voice present itself, I recognize it. I know without a shadow of a doubt that it is God speaking.

To hear God's voice, I had to have a desire to hear it. When I first started spending time in prayer, I did what most people do; I did all the talking. I would either get on my knees or lay prostrate on the floor and cry out to God. Immediately, afterward, I would get back up and go about my business. I didn't wait for an answer or an instruction from God. To be honest, I didn't think He would answer. However, as time went on, I realized there had to be more to praying.

The more time I spent in prayer, the more I realized I wanted to hear from God. As a result, I changed the way I approached God in prayer. I started to worship Him instead of rambling my requests first. I thanked Him. I invited His presence into my atmosphere. And I started to listen to Him.

After changing the way I entered into God's presence, I started to hear His voice. I would pray and then lay listening with spiritual ears for Him to speak. Sometimes, I heard nothing in return. While other times, my mind became flooded with answers. There were times I didn't like what I heard. But I embraced every word uttered. On some occasions, what I heard brought me to tears. At times, God shocked and amazed me. The more I heard, the more I wanted to hear from Him. The more I desired to hear from Him, the more I craved His presence. The more I craved His presence, the more I prayed. The more I prayed, the more He revealed to me.

When I became familiar with God's voice, I started to learn my spiritual gifts. Before hearing God's voice, I mostly prayed for myself or my family. However, when He spoke to me in prayer, He started to lead me on how to pray. The first noticeable change was the difference in the way I would cover myself and my family. I became aware of the attacks the devil planned to launch. Because of the shift in prayer, I was able to intercede and pray against the attacks. The Lord would not only speak to me, but He would use my mouth to command the enemy to flee. The more this happened, the more I became comfortable with God's voice.

The more I heard from God, the more I prayed. As my prayer life increased, the Lord also increased what He would reveal to me. God started to give me the names of people to pray for. He gave me the sicknesses, diseases, and the bondage to pray against. I was in complete awe with Him. Before hearing His voice, I didn't know or understand the importance of prayer in the life of a child of God. I underestimated the impact of His voice on my daily walk with Him.

Hearing God's voice is a crucial weapon during the season of waiting. God's voice will prepare you for the dangers ahead. God's voice will direct you in the right direction. God's voice will reveal the attacks of the enemy. God's voice will tell you what door not to open.

God's voice will expose the counterfeits. God's voice will tell you everything you need to know to sustain you during your season.

OBEDIENCE

1 Samuel 15:22~ And Samuel said, "Has the LORD as great delight in burnt offerings and sacrifices, as in obeying the voice of the Lord? Behold, to obey is better than sacrifice, and to listen than the fat of rams.

On my quest to gain a better understanding of obedience, I researched its meaning. During researching its meaning, I discovered obedience meant "an act or instance of obeying." To obey means "to follow the commands or guidance of; to conform to or comply with." Simply put, obedience to God meant to follow His instructions.

Although obeying God sounds as if it is easy, it is not. What I've discovered is that obeying God is a struggle and requires diligence. Obeying God will cause you pain at times. But obeying God is always worth it because though you struggle, the struggle is always worth that which you will ultimately gain through obedience.

Through trial and error, I learned the culprit behind struggling to obey was the flesh. The flesh works against the will of God. Romans 8:7 states *"For the mind that is set on flesh is hostile to God, for it does not submit to God's law; indeed, it cannot."* In other words, our flesh is unable to obey the instructions that the Lord gives because it does not have the ability to.

The primary reason that the flesh is unable to obey God is because no good thing lies within our flesh. Paul the Apostle tells us in Romans 7:18 *"For I know that nothing good dwells in me, that is, in my flesh. For I have the desire to do what is right, but not the ability to carry it out."* The things which God wants for us to do, and instructs us to do is always good. Because the instructions are always good, our flesh is in opposition to it and fights against it.

Another reason our flesh is unable to obey God is that it is always in direct opposition to the will of God. Galatians 5:17 states

"For the desires of the flesh are against the Spirit, and the desires of the Spirit, and the desires of the Spirit are against the flesh, for these are opposed to each other, to keep you from doing the things you want to do."

Though our flesh is naturally unwilling to follow the instruction of God, we can defeat it through prayer. Matthew 26:41 instructs us to *"Watch and pray that you may not enter into temptation. The spirit indeed is willing, but the flesh is weak."* Prayer is one of our most potent weapons because it, along with fasting, helps us to build our spirit. Building our spirit will help us overcome the struggle we face when walking in obedience to God.

Walking in obedience will assist us as we wait for the manifestation of God's promises. Walking in obedience allows the Lord to order our steps and direct our path. Walking in obedience ensures that we will always be protected because we will ultimately remain in the perfect will of God. Lastly, walking in obedience will result in us being blessed according to Deuteronomy 28:1-6:*"And if you faithfully obey the voice of the LORD your God, being careful to do all his commandments that I command you today, the LORD your God will set you high above all the nations of the earth. 2 And all these blessings shall come upon you and overtake you, if you obey the voice of the LORD your God. 3 Blessed shall you be in the city, and blessed shall you be in the field. 4 Blessed shall be the fruit of your womb and the fruit of your ground and the fruit of your cattle, the increase of your herds and the young of your flock. 5 Blessed shall be your baskets and your kneading bowl. 6 Blessed shall you be when you come in, and blessed shall you be when you go out."*

FAITH

Hebrews 11:1 (KJV) – Now faith is the substance of things hoped for, the evidence of things not seen.

Faith is defined as "a belief and trust in and loyalty to God." Or "firm belief in something for which there is no proof." Often times, believers use the word *faith* and even recite Hebrews 11:1 without searching for its true meaning. As a result, many wander through life holding on to something they cannot even grasp.

One must have a true understanding of what faith is while waiting for the manifestation of God's promise. Without a clear understanding of faith, one cannot truly obey, understand, or stand on the promises of God without wavering. Further, without faith, one won't be able to move pass unbelief towards something they could never see themselves doing.

It wasn't until I researched keywords within Hebrews 11:1 and developed true intimacy with God that I was able to grasp true faith. Through diligent research, I learned the word *substance* referred to "a physical material from which something is made or which has discrete existence." Also, I found *hope* is "the desire accompanied by expectation of or belief in fulfillment; or expectation of fulfillment or success." Lastly, I discovered *evidence* referred to "a visible sign of something." Simply put, faith means believing God even though there is nothing physically present to suggest that it exists. And faith is believing God despite all circumstances and odds pointing against that very thing happening.

Walking in true faith required me to develop a true intimate relationship with God. Growing up, I heard my grandparents speak highly of God. My grandmother told stories of having faith in God and God doing exactly what He had promised. Though I had knowledge of God being faithful to my grandmother, I needed to have the experience for myself. I had to seek God with all that I had and trust Him. I had to read God's word and get it in my heart. I had to literally fast and consecrate to help uproot the seeds of unbelief that I had. It wasn't an easy process. But the more I walked with God and allowed Him to work on me, the more my faith developed. The more I relied on God and lived according to His desires, the further faith in Him grew. The more I recited scriptures like Numbers 23:19—*"God is not a man, that he should lie, or a son of man, that he should change his mind. Has he said, and will he not do it? Or has he spoken, and will not he fulfill it?"* the more my faith increased. And ultimately, the more I walked in obedience and saw the manifestation of His word in my life, the more unwavering I became in my faith.

Building strong faith in God takes much diligence and dedication. Faith cannot be birth in you through the testimonies of others. Learning how to have faith in God cannot be accomplished by shortcuts. Faith in God only comes through having a consistent intimate relationship with God. Having undeniable faith in God is one of the vital pieces of your process of waiting on God as you walk with Him. So much so that His word says in Hebrews 11:6: *"And without faith, it is impossible to please him, for whoever would draw near to God must believe that he exists and that he rewards those who seek him."*

KNOW YOUR WORTH: YOU'RE VALUED AND MORE PRECIOUS THAN RUBIES

Proverbs 31:10 (KJV)- Who can find a virtuous woman? For her price is far above rubies.

Before living for Christ, my value depended on the number of friends I had, the clothes I wore, who I dated, the inches of my weaves, and the number of degrees I had. There I was, beautiful on the outside but dead on the inside. It wasn't until I truly surrendered to the Lord that I learned my true value.

One day, the Lord led me to Genesis 2. I had already read it a few times by now. I expected to read as I had before. I didn't expect for the Lord to open up my understanding like He did. I didn't expect to receive the revelation I had. That afternoon, the Lord took His time to teach me about the value He placed on women. First, the Lord led me through the familiar passages where He had formed man and every beast from the ground. He then pointed out the woman was the only creation He had created with the bone responsible for protecting vital organs in the chest—a rib. Also, the bone which is capable of regenerating itself after removal. As I continued to read the Lord's word, I truly understood, for the first time, the importance of what the Lord had done. The day God created Woman, He made a conscious decision to set women apart from His other creations.

The value women have goes far beyond being created with the rib of a man. This is evident by the Lord placing the value of a virtuous woman far above rubies. When I was of the world, I used to always say I was a "diamond," or at the very least, I pretended as though I was. At that time, I didn't even know making that very statement was devaluing my worth despite the fact that society tells women diamonds are valuable. Even though this is what the world has conditioned us to believe to be true, it's not.

When we compare ourselves to a diamond, we are diminishing our value. Rubies are actually more valuable than diamonds. When compared on a carat by carat basis, rubies are worth more than diamonds of similar size and weight. Also, unlike with diamonds, it's extremely rare and uncommon to find a huge ruby.

When I learned how valuable I was in Christ, I no longer accepted what I had accepted before. I no longer became thirsty or hungered for the wrong attention. I really started to understand because I was fearfully and wonderfully made, and as a woman; I was the gift. This revelation could not have come had I continued to be distracted by the cares and labels of this world. It could not have come to me had I not been undistracted as I waited on God.

THE BREAKING TO HEAL THE BROKEN

John 15:2~ Every branch in me that does not bear fruit, he takes away, and every branch that bears fruit, he prunes, that it may bear more fruit.

When I came to Christ, I was severely broken on the inside. I had experienced so much in my past. I had never truly healed. I was used to burying thoughts, feelings, and emotions for so long that I no longer realized there were broken pieces inside of me. I had somehow convinced myself I wasn't broken because those events, feelings, and heartaches no longer existed. I was allowed to live in this fantasy world until the Lord got me alone to Himself.

During my breaking process, the Lord started with my heart. At that time, I had been single for two years. I was happy just being with Jesus. I had no desire to be in a relationship with a man. As far as I was concerned, Jesus was all I wanted and needed. I had experienced the pain from my failed engagement and had no desire to risk being hurt again. I thought as long as I stayed with Jesus, and only Jesus, my heart was safe from being broken.

As I waited on God, He completely shattered my heart and put it back together again. The first step to the shattering of my heart was depositing the feeling of deep loneliness into it. The loneliness I felt was one that I had never felt before. During that time, I would go to sleep crying and wake up crying. I would pray and cry until I fell asleep. I was lost. I didn't understand why I was experiencing the heartache. I had lost myself in God and His word. In my mind, what I was experiencing made absolutely no sense. I wanted it to stop. I prayed for it to stop. But it seemed like the further I prayed for it to stop, the more intense the feeling became.

I can't tell you how long the breaking of my heart went on. But what I can tell you is that it was long enough for me to develop a routine. Every night, I put my daughters to bed, walked downstairs, lay on the living room floor, cried and prayed until I went to sleep. This cycle repeated itself until it came to an abrupt end.

After the painful cycle ended, it felt as though God had done surgery on my heart. It was as if He had carefully inspected each inch of my heart. He had removed every unnecessary piece attached to me. Every situation that had embedded itself in the grooves of my heart had been removed. The residue of the heartache from past relationships had been removed. Every split and broken areas were torn up and repaired. And at the end, my heart was healed and felt new.

After making my heart new, the next area the Lord dealt with was my lingering pride. My past had taught me to become self-sufficient and not to ask anyone for anything. It was to the point I was willing to go without before asking anyone for anything. I worked hard in school and at work to obtain positions and degrees that would make relying or being dependent on others unnecessary. As a result of this, I had become puffed up and absorbed with titles and material things. Ultimately, I had become unwilling to humble myself to anyone.

To break down my prideful ways, the Lord put me in situations where I had no other choice but to become humble and reach out to others for help. One Christmas, I had no money to buy my children gifts. My pride told me to cancel Christmas. I even convinced myself it was nothing wrong with my decision because my daughters were young and knew nothing about Christmas anyway. However, as soon as my mind had been made up, one of the evangelists from my church urged me to come to the upcoming toy giveaway. Initially, I assured her I didn't need to attend, but she continued to insist on me joining. It was as if God had revealed my situation to her because the more I declined her offer, the more she continued to encourage me to attend.

As a result of her persistence, the following Monday, I stood in line to get toys for my daughters. Before that moment, I never thought I would be in that position. I swallowed every ounce of pride I had as I waited. When it had been my turn, I pushed back the tears that were trying to form in the corners of my eyes and quickly picked out a few toys for my daughters.

Aside from this incident, God put me in other humbling situations. At that time, I hadn't been irresponsible with my money. Despite only purchasing necessities, I somehow did not have enough resources. During this season, I literally had to pick between purchasing necessities for myself or my children. Instead of putting my own needs first, I continued to put my children's needs first.

Over time, my shoes became extremely worn because I wore them every day. As a result of wearing them daily, holes formed in the bottom of them. I put cardboard or business cards in my shoes to keep my feet dry and warm during rainy and cold weather. Before that moment, I had never experienced anything like this.

Though I felt uncomfortable and broken at times, I became grateful and humble. I was grateful because I only had holes in the bottom of the shoe. I was filled with gratitude because I could still wear them. And I was thankful because my children didn't have to wear shoes with holes in them.

Had I not had those experiences, I would have remained prideful and puffed up. Had I not experienced them, I wouldn't know what it's like to go to bed hungry because you made sure your children had more than enough to eat. Had I not experienced the brokenness, I wouldn't be able to confidently proclaim the Lord to be my Jehovah Jireh.

SOUL TIES

1 Corinthians 6:16- Or do you not know that he who is joined to a prostitute becomes one body with her? For, as it is written, "The two shall become one flesh."

Soul ties are defined as a connection between two people in the soul realm. A soul tie can be either negative or positive. There are three different ways a soul tie can form—through close relationships; sexual relationships; or through promises, vows, or commitments.

A soul tie resulting from a close relationship can be either negative or positive. This type of soul tie can occur between people of the same gender or opposite gender. The soul tie happens because the individuals spend a lot of time together. As a result, there is a strong connection formed. This connection is strengthened over the duration of the relation.

The second soul tie occurs because of sexual intimacy between two people. This type of soul tie is formed any and every time there is intimacy. As a result of sexual soul ties, a person is prevented from moving forward when they are no longer intimate with that person. This type of soul tie often results in someone not being able to break free from the other person because their soul is continually being pulled back. Sexual soul ties are considered positive when it occurs between a man and woman in marriage because it results in the couple becoming one flesh. It is only negative when it happens outside of marriage.

The last and final type of soul tie occurs because of a vow, commitment, or promise made. In this situation, the soul tie is formed by words uttered from one's mouth. In the context of marriage, this type of soul tie is positive. However, in other instances, it only becomes negative when it causes a person to be trapped and tied to someone that is evil.

Prior to my decision to wait for the Lord to send my husband, I slept with whomever I pleased. At that time, I did not know of soul ties. Honestly, if I had known about them, I would have made the same decisions. My flesh controlled me and whatever spirit I had been tied to.

After surrendering my will to God, I no longer allowed my flesh to lead me. Anytime I became turned on by a lustful thought or a dream, I went into prayer instead of giving into it. I looked up scripture about temptation and would recite them over and over again until the thought or urge left. My favorite scripture to this day is 1 Corinthians 10:13 (ESV)- *"No temptation has overtaken you that is not common to man. God is faithful, and will not let you be tempted beyond your ability, but with the temptation he will also provide the way of escape, that you may be able to endure it."*

Even though I had quoted many scriptures, there had been times when I willfully decided to not take the way out of temptation. There were times when I allowed my flesh to rise and stay up. After being delivered from masturbation and all sexual soul ties, I became tied again. At that time, I had abstained from having sex for two years. I didn't intend on having sex. In fact, if I had been told I would do it, I would have laughed. I had been totally committed to waiting until I was married before having sex again. To help me on staying committed to abstaining until marriage, I learned all of my triggers. For example, I knew kissing anyone was off limits. I knew I couldn't watch movies or shows with sex scenes. I knew I couldn't engage in certain conversation. And I knew I definitely couldn't be alone with anyone behind closed doors.

For two years, I managed to be aware of my triggers and avoided them. Though it was difficult at times, I stood firm. When I broke my abstinence vow, it didn't happen suddenly. It was gradual. First, the guy and I started texting innocent flirty text messages. At the time, I knew I shouldn't have opened that door, but it felt good to be complimented. He said all of the right things. He made me blush and smile. He gave me butterflies. I started to crave his attention. Even though I knew it was wrong, I refused to slam that door shut; even when the Holy Spirit convicted me. Instead, I opened the door even more.

Over time, innocent text messages quickly turned into flirtatious phone calls. At that time, he knew I had been abstinent. Not only did he claim to be impressed with it, he also professed to have understood and respected my decision. I was naïve and let my guard completely down. I allowed him to come over to spend time with me. At first, everything remained innocent. We would talk and flirt with our eyes for hours without touching each other.

Soon, the late night talks tuned into steamy kissing sessions. I knew I was playing with fire. I knew I was wrong. I knew kissing was a huge trigger for me, but I continued to do it. I knew it caused me to lust after him, but I kept kissing. I even convinced myself *nothing* else would happen. *Boy,* was I wrong!

Ultimately, the kissing led to touching, massaging, and then him performing oral sex. When everything was happening, I couldn't concentrate on anything else. I wasn't thinking logically or soundly. I was just thinking about pleasing my flesh at all costs.

After each encounter, I regretted what I had done. I would immediately cry after each climax. He would apologize and comfort me. After he would leave, I would cry out and pray. I promised God I wouldn't allow him over again. During those moments, I meant every word. Even though I knew I wanted God more than I wanted him, I couldn't stop.

No matter how hard I tried to say "no," I couldn't. I tried to convince myself I was strong enough to resist him, but I wasn't. I would even tell him after each encounter that it would never happen again. However, no matter how much I tried to resist him, my body craved him. I couldn't turn away from the sin I had been committing. I couldn't close the door. When I tried, every area of my life became negatively affected. I couldn't concentrate at work. My mind started to taunt me with thoughts of him pleasing me. I had become a wreck internally. I no longer had the strength to stop, so I continued to give in.

Months after kissing and engaging in oral sex, we had sex. That night, I listened to the thoughts that had often played in my mind while

I was with him. I didn't tell myself "no" like I had done previously. This time, I didn't tell myself I would regret it later. I didn't tell myself God would be displeased with me. I didn't remind myself I had been saving myself for marriage. At that moment, I could care less about my future husband. I just gave in and allowed him inside of me.

Immediately, I felt a surge within. I felt extremely lustful. I felt heat all around me. I opened myself up as much as I could. I was taken over with lust and perversion. I no longer cared about anything but pleasing my flesh and experiencing what I had been experiencing.

As soon as things ended, I felt a major difference in my spirit. I felt rage. I felt anger. I was extremely conflicted. I no longer felt the peace I felt before allowing him inside of me. Instantly, I knew something was wrong. At the time, I didn't know what had occurred in the spirit realm. All I had known was that I had made a major mistake. I was unmarried and no longer abstinent!

After that night, I continued to have sex with him. I tried as hard as I could to resist him but couldn't. Each time, I tried to talk myself out of it but was unsuccessful. Now, I felt weak when it came to him. I felt as though we had this major connection. My body craved his like never before. I felt as though I had taken a hit of some drug and had become hooked. I felt as though I was being controlled and couldn't stop what was happening.

During that time, I changed internally. I had anger fits and couldn't explain them. I had really bad mood swings. I was a complete wreck on the inside and struggled really hard to keep what I had felt from manifesting itself on the outside.

I really tried to maintain my relationship with God as much as possible. I still went to church as usual; I still read my Bible. But I couldn't pray the same. I had become too ashamed to communicate with God. I constantly felt convicted. I knew I was wrong but couldn't stop fornicating and lusting after him.

As time went on, I became secretly depressed. I literally felt as though I was being pulled in two different directions. I wanted the same level of intimacy I had months prior, but I also wanted intimacy from this guy. I once again found myself in a bad place. The only difference this time was my flesh felt too strong for me to control.

The strength of my flesh wasn't just a feeling. It was a reality. When the Lord cleansed me the first time, the spirits I had been tied to for years were gone. When I decided to engage in sexual activity after being cleansed, the spirits came back stronger. For a few months, I continued to have sex with him on a regular basis. I continued to feel out of control. I continued to have different spirits deposited into my spirit from him. I didn't know how to get a grip on the urges and feelings I had.

It wasn't until I finally decided I had enough. I was tired of sinning against God. I was tired of feeling like trash. I became tired of feeling out of control on the inside. I did the only thing I knew to do; I finally repented with my entire heart. After repenting, I fought against my flesh. I talked myself out of answering his phones calls. I ignored every text message he sent. Eventually, before completely changing my number, I placed his number on the block list and stayed on my face in prayer.

I wish I could tell you the process of being re-delivered was easy. I wish I could say to you "soul ties" weren't real. But I can't, they are real. I had to fight harder than I've ever fought in my life to be delivered from the soul tie I had with him. At that time, I didn't know why the fight was extremely hard until I came across Luke 11:24-26 which states: *"When the unclean spirit has gone out of a person, it passes through waterless places seeking rest, and finding none, it says, 'I will return to my house from which I came.' And when it comes, it finds the house swept and put in order. Then it goes and brings seven other spirits more evil than itself, and they enter and dwell there. And the last state of that person is worse than the first."*

Even though the process of being re-delivered was excruciating at times, it was well worth it. Had I continued on the path I was on with him, I wouldn't be as close to God as I am. Had I continued down that path, I wouldn't be sitting here writing these very words. And even worse, I wouldn't be set free and delivered!

LEARNING AND UNDERSTANDING PURPOSE

Jeremiah 29:11- For I know the plans I have for you," declares the LORD,
'Plans to prosper you and not to harm you, plans to give you hope and a future.

Purpose is defined as being "the reason for which something exists or is done." Everyone was born with a purpose. There is absolutely no human being born without a purpose. And what's amazing is when the Lord created us, He created us with our own unique, one of a kind, purpose.

Many people are walking aimlessly around the world trying to find their purpose. You may even be one of them. Honestly, for many years, I was one. In college, I pursued two college degrees because I wasn't certain of my purpose. I worked many jobs, some dead end, in search of my purpose. It wasn't until I surrendered my will to God that my purpose was revealed to me. The revelation didn't come overnight. The revelation collided with my own plans for my life. This revelation of what my purpose was could not have been revealed to me until I had completely surrendered my life, will, and ways to God.

As I look back, I realize each act of me surrendering my will to God drew me closer to His purpose for my life. The more time I spent in God's word, I became closer to my purpose. The further I spent time in prayer listening to God's voice, the more my ears became inclined to hear God's voice concerning my purpose. And the more I learned about my true worth, the further I was ready to hear God's purpose for my life.

Without being in a surrendered state, true purpose cannot be found. God's purpose for our lives is far greater than what we could have ever imagined. It's bigger than our biggest dreams. It requires us to have faith in God's will. It needs us to believe the impossible is possible. It requires us to takes leaps of faith far beyond what we could have ever imagined. It requires us to trust God with every ounce of our beings.

I thought my purpose on this earth was to work as an attorney. I didn't see myself doing anything else beyond the courtroom. It wasn't until I submitted to the Lord, allowed Him to break me down and build me back up that God started to reveal my purpose to me. I literally had to be not just saved but filled with the Holy Spirit and working the gifts that were placed inside of me to find out. Pursuing my God-given purpose required me to think beyond my own limitations and abilities. Pursuing my purpose required, and still requires me to follow every instruction God gives to me.

It wasn't until I fasted and prayed for three days that the Lord revealed part of my purpose to me. After my fast ended, I was woken up at 6 am. The Lord told me I was to form a motivational speaking company. He instructed me to also write a book. Before that moment, I never had the desire to be a business owner or write a book. But because I had already surrendered to God, I knew my only choice was to do as He said despite what I thought or felt. He was my King. He was my creator and knew my purpose.

After executing the first set of instructions, the Lord revealed more to me. The Lord sent reliable prophets to explain the things He had already shown me. They helped me to understand what the Lord was doing in my life. To sum everything up, the Lord had decided from the foundation of this earth I would travel the world, preaching, teaching, and speaking. I was stunned. I was a little afraid. I was a nervous wreck because, at that time, I wasn't ordained as anything though I knew what gifts the Lord had given me. I understood the call on my life, but I didn't expect God had created me with such great purpose and authority.

I knew I was unworthy, but I knew I had no other choice but to say yes to the Lord's plan for my life. I had spent too many years of my life walking in disobedience. I had asked God to use me as His vessel for a long time. I told the Lord to send me wherever and I would go.

Had I not already been in a surrendered state waiting for the Lord to reveal His purpose for my life, I would have rejected it. His plan is unbelievable. His plan is far beyond mine. His plan has required me to accept the reality that I may never step foot in a courtroom to practice law again. As difficult as this was to swallow, I've grown comfortable with this reality because *"God is not man, that he should lie, or a son of man, that he should change his mind. Has he said, and will he not do it? or has he spoken, and will he not fulfill it?"* (Number 23:19).

Though I am still waiting for the full manifestation of His plan, I continue to walk in obedience and follow each instruction He gives me. I continue to stay humble and at His feet in prayer. And I continue to believe at the appointed time everything promised will come to pass as long as I continue to walk in pursuit of His purpose.

OVERCOMING THE OPINIONS OF PEOPLE

Jeremiah 1:8- Do not be afraid of them, for I am with you to deliver you, declares the LORD.
Isaiah 51:7- Listen to me, you who know righteousness, the people in whose heart is my law; fear not the reproach of man, nor be dismayed at their revilings.

What I've discovered on my journey with Christ and while waiting for the manifestation of God's promises is that others will not always understand or support you. The truth is, some people will become jealous and envious of who God is molding you into being. The hard reality is, everyone, including family and longtime friends, won't always rejoice with you. One of the biggest reason is because some people want you to stay bound. Some don't want you to get more attention than they have. Perhaps your growth and life make them feel uncomfortable because it may remind them that they aren't doing what God has called them to do. Instead of getting upset or even allowing this to stop or deter you, use it as fuel to keep going.

Everyone who is around you, family included, is not for you. I know it hurts. I know it's unbelievable. I know it doesn't make sense. But God already knew it would happen when He created you. The Lord knew who would come up against you before they formed the thought. The Lord actually allowed it. Crazy Right? Not at all! In the Book of Job, the Lord gave Satan permission to try Job. During that time, Job's friends and own wife voiced their opinions to him that were contrary to the will of God for his life. At that time, God knew no matter what the devil did to Job, no matter how bad things got, no matter who would turn against Job, no matter what they would say about or to him, and no matter what the devil tried, Job would still serve Him. The Lord knew Job (though he experienced momentary weakness) would ultimately be strengthened.

Just like in the case of Job, the Lord allows people to even tempt and test us with their opinions. He does so because He knows that we will stand in the end as long as we hold on to Him. The Lord uses the criticism and opinions of others to test our loyalty to Him. He uses others to see if we have truly been delivered from different things. Even though it seems harsh, it's all for our good. How? God knows when we are tested by the opinions of others, He has already equipped us with the necessary skills and tools to pass the test. He's confident we can pass it if we apply the knowledge we've gained. All we must do is stand and not give up or give in to the opinions and criticism of others, as we allow the Lord to work things out.

When we ignore the opinions and criticism of others, the Lord takes care of things for us. Exodus 14:14 tells us *"The Lord will fight for you, and you have only to be still."* When we know we are living according to the Lord's instructions; He's obligated to handle everyone who comes up against us. We must stand still and trust that He's going to do it!

No matter what anyone says about you, you must hold on to God and His word. The attacks are meant to push you further into your destiny and further into your purpose. Instead of giving in and acting the fool, pray for them and their opinions concerning you. Also, pray to the Lord to deliver you from the opinions of others. Also, meditate on 2 Corinthians 4:8-10: *We are afflicted in every way, but not crushed; perplexed, but not driven to despair; persecuted, but not forsaken; struck down, but not destroyed; always carrying in the body the death of Jesus so that the life of Jesus may also be manifested in our bodies."*

PERSECUTION

Persecution is "to harass or punish in a manner designed to injure, grieve, or afflict; specifically: to cause to suffer because of belief or: to annoy with persistent or urgent approaches (such as attacks, please, or importance)." Persecution in the life of a believer is a common thing even though teaching on it has been totally or partially abandoned. This has led to many believers caving in or falling away when they experience persecution. This has also resulted in many assuming and wholeheartedly believing that one isn't living upright before God or God doesn't care about them. As a result, many believers aren't adequately prepared to go through their process of longsuffering; and this results in their inability to reign with Christ as He desires.

Prior to being completely surrendered to Christ, I suffered persecution. I had others not only slander my name but harass me in many others ways. At that time, I remained unconcerned no matter how much it occurred. To be honest, I actually felt as though the attention I received through persecution was because I was doing everything right. The persecution I experienced did not hurt my feelings nor did I lose any sleep over it.

After submitting to Christ, the persecution I experienced hurt me to the core. After being obedient and releasing my first book, *Confessions of An OverComer: From Tragedy to Triumph*, I suffered the worse persecution that I've ever experienced since being saved. Before releasing the book, I knew that I would be persecuted because God had told me. However, I didn't expect it to shake me as it had.

During that season of persecution, many things occurred. I had family members harass me via social media and telephone. They did not want to accept the reality that one of our cousins had, in fact, molested me when I was four years old. I was told that I had lied. I was called a false prophet. I was told I was unsaved and was full of the devil. To make matters worse, one of my aunts went through my family spreading rumors and lies. I was horrified. I couldn't believe what I had been experiencing.

The persecution I experienced did not stop there. Others began making remarks and attempts to stop me from advancing. I literally felt as though God had led me into the middle of the battlefield to be attacked. It seemed as though I had snakes on all sides of me. God started to show me the true intentions of others. People whom I had known for years and thought loved me didn't. I was crushed. I cried many tears. The feeling of loneliness started to creep in again. My heart felt as though acid was poured on it. At times, my insides felt as though they were on fire. However, as bad as I felt, God still comforted me.

Although I knew the persecution was coming, there was nothing to prepare me for its pain. A week before it all started, the Holy Spirit kept uttering "stand and see the salvation of the Lord. If you hold your peace, the Lord will fight your battle." At that time, I knew it had to be very close because of the frequency of the utterance. I found myself praying and hoping it would pass quickly. I knew it was going to happen and there was nothing I could do about it. I knew that it was inevitable even though I was afraid. All I could do was pray to bring me comfort.

The more I prayed to God, the more He reminded me I had all of the necessary tools to stand during the persecution. He even jogged my memory of a word I had released entitled "Remnant, Persecution Is Your Portion." At the time I delivered that word, I had no idea I was preaching to myself. I was shocked! I wanted to hide from the revelation God had given me. I tried to hide from my very own words because they cut so deep, deeper than the words of the persecutor. But I knew deep down I couldn't.

Ultimately, instead of hiding, I picked up the notes from the sermon and allowed them to speak to me. Whenever the question of why must I go through persecution arose, I heard 2 Timothy 3:12, which states: *"Indeed all who desire to live a godly life in Christ Jesus will be persecuted."* When I needed direction as to what to do in the midst of persecution, I was reminded of 1 Peter 4:12-14: *"Beloved, do not be surprised at the fiery trial when it comes upon you to test you, as though something strange were happening to you. But rejoice insofar as you share Christ's suffering that you may also rejoice and be glad when his glory is revealed. If you are insulted for the name of Christ, you are blessed, because the Spirit of glory and of God rests upon you."* And when I needed peace and comfort, I read 2 Corinthians 4:8-10: *"We are afflicted in every way, but not crushed; perplexed, but not driven to despair; persecuted; but not forsaken, struck done, but not destroyed, always carrying in the body the death of Jesus, so that the life of Jesus may also be manifested in our bodies."*

Worship, prayer, and the word of God brought me the most strength during my season of persecution. I would recite the words regarding persecution to myself as often as I needed. I prayed with much intensity. I asked God to have mercy on all of those who persecuted me with their words and actions. And I sang worship songs until the feeling of hurt and pain passed.

Although there was pain during my season of persecution, there was also spiritual growth. My spiritual vision became so clear that I could see snakes as they stood in front of me speaking. I started to have the ability to hear what others would say before they said it. My visions and dreams became clearer. I started to love people to the point that I still remained kind and loving towards them though God had exposed that they did not like me. I literally started to identify more with Christ in many remarkable ways.

Even though persecution does not feel well, I must admit that it is necessary. I wish I can tell you that the season of persecution is over for me, it's not. As I type these very words, it has not changed. However, the way I look at persecution has changed. I now hold the view, as long as God offered me up for persecution, it is for my good. Although it doesn't feel good on some days, it still has a positive impact. Because people are talking about me, I am receiving free advertisement. People who would not have read my book otherwise are reading my book. The persecution in my life is resulting in the Lord being glorified more and more. And it is leading to me being strengthened during the process.

OVERCOMING NEGATIVE THOUGHTS WHILE WAITING

2 Corinthians 10:5(KJV)- Casting down imaginations, and every high thing that exalteth itself against the knowledge of God, and bringing into captivity every thought to the obedience of Christ.
Isaiah 26:3 You keep him in perfect peace whose mind is stayed on you, because he trusts in you.

Our adversary, the devil, has no power over us. He plants seeds in our minds to attempt to have us believe the opposite of what the Lord wants us to believe. There were many times that I had (and still have) to speak scripture over my mind as I waited. The enemy was constantly attempting to plant seeds in my mind to distract me. There were days where I would ignore the pull of the Holy Spirit to write or even study the word of God because of the seeds planted. There were moments I listened to the devil and told God I couldn't do what He called me to do. In those moments, I was blinded. I gave in to the negative thoughts. I allowed them to take root in my mind. During those times, I became afraid and stood still.

To overcome my negative thoughts and opinions, I had to cast the thoughts out of my mind. When thoughts entered my mind, I started to place them underneath the subjection of Christ. To do this, I would recite scripture to the contrary of my negative thoughts. For example, whenever I felt I wasn't good enough, I recited Psalms 139:14~ *I praise you, for I am fearfully and wonderfully made. Wonderful are your works; my soul knows it very well."* During the times I felt as though God made a mistake by giving me my purpose, I recited *Jeremiah 29:11*(NIV)~ *For I know the plans I have for you, declared the LORD, "plans to prosper you and not to harm you, plans to give you hope and a future."* Also, in those moments when fear controlled my mind, I recited *2 Timothy*

1:7(KJV)~For God hath not given us the spirit of fear, but of power, and of love and of a sound mind."

Whenever I couldn't read or was in need of more encouragement, I worshipped God. In those moments, I turned on worship music and sung at the top of my lungs, or I wept as I listened to whatever song that played. Sometimes, I would even revisit the songs that got me through the previous season to help me remember all the great things God had *already* brought me through. I repeated this as many times as needed. I reiterated this until I felt freedom and negative thoughts were replaced with peace and joy.

If I were not in an environment that allowed me to sing or weep, I would put on my earphones and just listen to the words being sung by various artists. In those moments, I listened until my spirit stirred. There were sometimes when I had to step away to the restroom for a brief moment to cry. Afterwards, I would return to whatever I was doing and continue to listen to the lyrics of the song until my negative thoughts escaped.

Had I not spent more time focusing on God like I had, I would not have been able to overcome the negative thoughts. My emotions would have been everywhere like they had previously been. But because God was, and still is, omnipresent—everywhere and accessible at any time—I was able to recover quicker from every mental breakdown, by casting my cares upon Him. Because of this, depression, low self-esteem, fear, and anxiety were no longer able to take root in my mind.

WORKING WHILE WAITING

Colossians 3:23-24(NIV)- Whatever you do, work as it with all your heart, as working for the Lord, not for human masters. 24 since you know that you will receive an inheritance from the Lord as a reward. It is the Lord Christ you are serving.
Matthew 5:15- Nor do people light a lamp and put it under a basket, but on a stand, and it gives light to all in the house.

When the Lord told me to leave my ex-fiancé in 2013, I didn't listen. I ignored what He said even though I had prayed for His help to get me out of the situation. It wasn't until January 2014 that I followed His instructions. By that time, the Lord refused to open any doors for me. I was lost and distraught. I felt like the Lord didn't want me to be happy even though the person I was trying to marry wasn't any good for me. He cheated on me several times, had children with other women, and didn't help me to support the children I had with him. Yet and still, I held on to him out of fear of being a single mother.

After almost an entire year of walking in disobedience, I decided to listen to the voice of the Lord. Before listening, I tried to bargain with the Lord out of fear. I cried out to God and told Him how much pain I would be in. I actually tried to convince God, the one who knows the number of hairs on my head, that my plan was the best for my life. The entire time I tried to convince Him, the Lord continued to reassure me that I would be fine. As a result, I finally left my ex-fiancé and became a single mother of two diaper-wearing babies.

After leaving him, I was instructed by God to wait for Him to send me my husband. To even solidify the request made, the Lord not only allowed me to have a dream of my husband on our wedding day, He sent many to confirm what He had already told me. At that time, I had no problem waiting on God to send my mate because I needed to be healed. I also needed to be delivered from lust, fornication, as well as other things. And more importantly, I needed to find my identity I had lost over time.

As I waited, I thought I had everything figured out. I turned down all advances anyone made towards me. I didn't really go out anywhere besides to work, church, and shopping. I thought I was winning because I refused to let a man in.

It wasn't until two years into my wait the Lord revealed to me I had been waiting incorrectly. I assumed as long as I wasn't fornicating or dating, I was on the right track, but I wasn't. Yes, I had been going to church faithfully. And I was working in my local church a little bit. But God revealed to me I wasn't working as He desired. Because I literally sat at home waiting for this mysterious man to show up and sweep me off my feet.

The morning the Lord burst my bubble, He woke me up early. As I laid in my bed looking up at the ceiling, I decided to pick up my Bible to read. I couldn't fall back to sleep. My daughters were sound asleep. It was only 5 am, and they wouldn't be getting up for a while. As I reached for my Bible, I decided to just flip it open and start reading. To my surprise, the Bible opened up to the book of Ruth. Immediately, I knew God was speaking.

As I read Ruth, the Lord almost immediately started to minister to me. First, He rebuked me for not working in His Kingdom. As I read, He pointed out how Ruth was found working. She wasn't just waiting for someone to come get her. She placed herself in position to be found. The Lord directed me to get to work in His kingdom. At first, I was like "*what?*! But I am working in my local church." The Lord repeated His instruction. But this time, He followed with "your husband will find you working just like Boaz found Ruth working." I was stunned. Before that morning, I had never noticed or even considered that I wasn't in the position to be found by my husband-to-be.

After that morning, I got to work in God's kingdom. At the instruction of God, I co-founded My Sister's Keeper— Save Our Souls, a Christian woman's organization that encouraged women to live lives that are holy and acceptable to Christ. I continued to teach my church's youth as a youth leader. I continued to work in the nursery on Sunday mornings. I started posting videos ministering to others on my social media accounts. I became a prayer warrior for my church and prayed almost every Friday morning on its prayer line. I went out with my church's street witnessing ministry. I launched a YouTube channel devoted solely to releasing God inspired messages. And I stepped out and spoke as a motivational speaker.

From that one conversation with God, I learned about working while waiting. When God desires for us to wait for Him to do something for us, He expects us to grow during the process. God wants us to explore who we are. He doesn't envision us shutting down and hiding. He doesn't want to force change upon us; He wants us to partner with Him in the process. He wants to pour in the attributes we need. God wants us to be willing to be pruned when necessary. He wants us to serve others as if serving Him. God wants us to work in His kingdom and on ourselves as we wait!

THE MANIFESTATION OF THE WAIT…OH WAIT!

After remaining single for a little over three years, the Lord sent someone into my life. Though I had been waiting for him to come, I doubted he was sent by God. Everything about our connection was unexpected. For example, he lived in Florida while I lived in California. He was a few years younger than I was but had a lot of spiritual wisdom. He wasn't my preference either. I wasn't attracted to him physically, although he wasn't ugly. And I wasn't too fond of the way he dressed. Based on these things, I felt the Lord had laughed at my list of wants and gave me the complete opposite.

Even though I knew and heard what the Lord said concerning him, I still tried to run in the opposite direction. The first few conversations between the two of us were friendly. We talked a lot about God, prophecy, and surface things about our lives. At that time, there was no interest in him because I thought the connection was for friendship purposes only. Prior to meeting him, I had been praying to be connected to men and women who were also sold out. I thought he was an answer to that prayer.

It wasn't until I felt his spirit that I realized the connection was more than I had prayed for. His spirit felt too familiar. It felt like the spirit I had felt during prayer before we met. Instantly, I tried to rationalize what I had felt. But I was unable to. To comfort my mind, I strived to ignore the feeling. I didn't want him to be the one. Unfortunately, the more I ignored them, the more intense the feelings became. I couldn't deny what I felt even though I still tried.

After being in denial for a few days, I was forced to face the truth. On the night in question, I was experiencing severe back pain after I had called someone and prayed for them. After collapsing on my bed, I prayed for the Lord to strengthen my body. I recall crying myself to sleep that night because of the pain. I was exhausted. I laid on the bed that night struggling as I went in and out of sleep. I lay in bed with a full face of makeup and work clothes still on. Each time I woke, I tried to get up but could not. I kept praying that God would give me the strength I needed to get up.

After praying several times, I heard my phone signal that I had a text message. As I struggled to reach for my phone, I said: "*Lord, help me.*" As I read the text message, I realized the text was from him. The text simply said, "Can I call you?" My response was "yes." I didn't know what to expect from the call. I was hoping I would be able to stay awake long enough to force myself out of bed. When he called, I quickly answered the phone. After he greeted me, he explained how the Lord woke him up and instructed him to call and pray for me. I was shocked and grateful at the same time.

As he prayed for me, I could literally feel the pain leaving my body. As he prayed, astonishment covered my mind. I had not told him where the pain had been. I had not even told him I was in pain. But he knew. That night, he left no stone unturned. By the end of him praying, my body was completely restored to the position it had been in prior to me covering the individual I had covered in prayer.

I wasn't accustomed to what I had experienced. Before that moment, the Lord had not allowed me to connect with anyone on that level. I had never had a man cover me in that way. Instead of accepting what happened occurred as being anything more than a spiritual connection, I brushed it off again.

The next morning, I woke up to instructions from God for me to cover him later that night. I told God: "What!? Now you know this is somebody else's husband. I'll do it because you said so." Throughout the entire day, I questioned God over and over again. I honestly didn't feel comfortable covering him. I had no issue with praying for others, but *this* was just a little different. It was a little too intimate for me. When it became apparent the Lord wasn't going to change His mind; I decided I was going to obey Him.

After putting my children to sleep, he called. I answered the phone with a knot in my throat. We greeted each other. He asked me how my day had been. I told him it was fine. He then told me that he was going to use wisdom that night and go to sleep early. I could hear the tiredness in his voice. I replied that I understood but asked if it was okay for me to pray for him. He stated "yes." That night, I covered him as God led me. After I had finished praying, he thanked me and told me God had told him earlier that I would be praying for him. Wait! *What* is what I thought. God had set me up and told him about it. Instantly, I thought *"God, I'm going to need for you not to tell my business."* My only response to him was *"really?"* He went on to tell me he was grateful for our connection because he had prayed for a woman who could cover him in prayer. I was shocked. *Wayment!!* was what I thought. He continued to speak. He said he was the one always doing the covering. My only response was "wow, that's crazy." He then proceeded to tell me that the prayer had brought strength to him. He thanked me, and we hung up the phone.

I sat there that night asking God what was really going on. He was a nice guy, but I wasn't interested in him. Spiritually, he was what I had prayed for, but I wasn't attracted to him. Confused and concerned, I prayed that night that the connection would not go beyond what it was.

The following night, the Lord woke me up. As soon as I shifted in my bed before I even opened my eyes, I heard the lyrics "my storage is empty" followed by a glimpse of his face. God then instructed me to call him and pray. I was like *"really God!!"* I was confused. I again told the Lord it wasn't proper for me, someone else's future wife, to be covering someone else's future husband. God repeated the instruction to call and pray for him again. *Ugh!* I whimpered as I reached for my phone and dialed pressed on his name. When he answered, I explained to him what had just occurred. After I finished speaking, he replied "okay." Again, I prayed everything the Lord told me to pray. After I finished praying, he thanked me. He told me he was, in fact, feeling empty. I, sitting straight up in my bed with wide eyes, was completely stunned.

The next day, he flooded my phone with sweet text messages. I was flattered. I thanked him and went about my day. Later that night, he asked if I had asked God about our connection. I told him "No. It's not any of my business." He now said "how can two walk together if they don't agree?" I sat there and rolled my eyes as I told him again "it's not any of my business." I then said that I wasn't asking God anything because He would let me know. That was not a good enough response for him because He continued to speak. As he spoke, he revealed the things I had told God earlier that day. He stated: "You asked God whether this was a distraction because you are fasting. You asked whether I was a counterfeit. You asked God what is this." I sat on the other end of the phone upset and shocked! God told him my business again. I didn't like it at all. I felt for whatever reason, God was against me and was on his side.

To settle the matter, I came up with the perfect solution. With this, I would be able to prove to God that he was, in fact, a counterfeit. I told him I needed to fast and pray for three days. I was confident that he would abandon the idea of anything being between us over that period. To my surprise and bewilderment, he responded: "*Wow*! God told me you would say this. I just didn't expect that it would be this soon. Instead of not talking for three days, how about we do not talk for five days?" I replied "okay" with excitement. In my mind, things were going perfectly. That night, we hung up the phone, committed to not interacting with each other for the next five days.

The following morning, I woke up feeling as if the fast period would be a piece of cake. I didn't anticipate that things were going to be difficult. I barely knew him. We had talked every day for several days, but that was it. I enjoyed the conversations we had because his revelation was amazing!! I did not think he had made such an impact on my life in a short amount of time. I felt I had everything under control.

As I drove to work that morning; I called my best friend, Colbie. I intended to tell her everything that had occurred. I thought she would side with me. I thought she would say to me how out of the pocket he was for even suggesting our connection was anything more than being a brother and sister-in-Christ. To my surprise, Colbie didn't support me. In fact, she had a logical rebuttal for every single one of my complaints. She even dared to tell me God wasn't going to bring fire from the sky as I had asked as a sign he was the one. She continued, "After these five days, I'm going to need for you to have several seats." *What!?* I thought. I knew deep down she was right. But I wasn't going to admit it. I wanted what I wanted, and that was it.

Even though I knew Colbie was right, I needed to seek godly counsel from one other person, Rachel. Rachel always gave me the right words to make sense of everything. She is actually the one who pushed me to prophesy when I was afraid to walk in my calling. That morning, as I sat with her, explaining everything, she listened. After I finished speaking, she lifted her arm in front of my face. The hairs on her arm were standing straight up. She said: "Girl, if you don't stop playing. Weren't you just asking and praying for manifestation. Here it is, and you're playing." *Ugh!* I grumbled. Even the prophetess was against me. After a brief conversation, as I walked away, she told me: "The Holy Spirit is going to tell you when to reach out to him. You're not going five days without talking to him. You better be obedient when the Holy Spirit tells you." I replied "okay," as I walked away feeling defeated. It seemed like I was the only one who felt fasting and not talking to him was the right decision. I was the only one who felt he was nothing more than a distraction.

Even though I didn't have support from anyone else, I continued to fast. The first few hours of the fast were breezy. After the last conversation I had about him, I didn't think of him anymore. However, by the afternoon, my flesh started to kick my butt. I became extremely weak. I felt as though layers of my heart were being peeled away. I felt as though my spirit was lighter. Complete confusion set in. I started to yarn from him and didn't like the feeling. I began to pray. I begged God to step in and stop what I was feeling. After praying and praying, the small still voice of the Lord told me I needed to soften up and stop running. *Wait, what!* was what ran through my mind. I countered "but God, you know he's a counterfeit." The only response I got back was to go with the flow of what was happening. At that moment, I wanted to run off kicking and screaming, but I knew better. I knew I had to ultimately listen to God. Unfortunately, I decided it still wasn't time to go with the flow. I kept fasting from him and food.

That first night of fasting from him, I listened to sermons. One of the sermons I listened to really gave me clarity because it involved the discussion or counterfeits vs. god-sent mates. As I listened to the sermon, I evaluated the guy I had been trying to fast away. As I listened to the characteristics of the counterfeit, I realized he hadn't displayed any of them. In fact, he seemed to be the total opposite of a fake. That night, I decided I was going to just allow time to tell me what I should do. If he were, in fact, a counterfeit, he would change as time went on. I went to sleep that night knowing, though I would continue the fast, I would allow him to pursue me without the dramatics of me trying to beat him off.

The next morning, I woke up at 4 am. I was slightly frustrated because I wanted to sleep more. As I lay in bed, I listened to the silence. I knew God wanted to speak to me. I knew it was the only explanation for why I suddenly woke up when I was resting so soundly. After about five minutes of laying in complete silence, God started to speak. He instructed me to send him a text message apologizing for being stubborn. The only thought I had was "*I ain't gonna do it.*" I ignored the instruction and tried to unsuccessfully go back to sleep. As expected, God would not allow me to go back to sleep. After tossing and turning for what seemed like an eternity, I reached for my phone and started texting him the forced apology.

I held my breath as I waited for a response. I honestly didn't expect for him to respond. I know if I were in his position, I would not have answered. To my surprise, he responded almost immediately. He accepted my apology. I was relieved. In that moment, my heart softened towards him. I had an urge to be transparent with him about what I had felt the previous day. I went to my notepad and sent him the note I wrote that afternoon as I experienced the agony of not talking to him. The note read: *"Dear J, So today is day one of this five-day fast from you. This morning, I thought it would be easy, but it's not. My spirit feels a little empty. My heart feels a little lighter. I'm not understanding how someone can just come into your life and change the atmosphere within your heart in almost an instant. I have these urges to call or text you. Urges to send you emojis. My heart needs to hear the comforting tone of your voice, but I have not been granted the permission to reach out. As the hours go by, my heart is softened more towards you. I don't know what the future holds. I'm nervous and scared. I don't know what to expect. I've been praying for God to work on my exposed areas that will only hinder and not advance His will. I've been praying for God to lead me on how to let go and allow everything to flow as He desires. I'm praying…."* His response shocked me. He said, *"Wow,* I felt the same way." He then admitted that not talking to a woman had never affected him as it had in this instance. I was relieved to know I wasn't the only one who felt this way.

That morning, we decided we would text and still not talk for another day. I tried to only text him, but it wasn't enough for me. I was also really hungry. I wanted to throw in the towel. I understood I couldn't fast him away. I was now willing to be obedient to what God said. I still didn't like it though. I knew it would take time for me to totally submit to God's desire. It would take time for me to be comfortable with going with the flow.

At the end of day two, I texted him and asked for him to explain why we weren't talking on the phone. I was over not talking to him by now. Instead of answering me, he asked me a series of questions which I had to answer. I was annoyed because I felt he was being complicated. But I understood why he was asking the questions. He wanted to make sure that I wouldn't try to fast him away the next week or in the future. He also wanted to make sure that we were on the same page as well. After answering his questions to his liking, he called me.

The conversation following the fast was a lot different from the discussions before the fast. The previous chats were friendly. The talks that occurred now were more of, *okay, let me get to really know you.* I had become willing to let him in. I now knew God placed him in my life. I knew though he wasn't my preference, he was part of my purpose. And I knew we had to take our time to build a strong foundation based on friendship before anything.

Even though I knew all signs pointed to him being the one, I still had a little uncertainty. He just didn't look like the man I had seen in dreams or visions. Granted, I never remembered the facial features. But there were too many inconsistencies for me to swallow. My dreams and visions had been accurate in the past when they would manifest. Things just weren't adding up for me. For example, he was too short. His skin tone was darker than the man I always saw in my dreams and visions. And his stature was off too.

I pushed back against him until God stopped me dead in my tracks. As I pointed out the differences to Him, God gently said: "He's your husband." I asked God: "How? He doesn't add up to the dreams and visions you have shown me for the last 3.5 years." The Lord kept saying, "It's him." I felt in my spirit there was something more to the story. But because it was God who told me, I pushed my apprehension aside and said, "Okay God."

From the moment I said okay to God concerning him being my husband, unexplainable things started to happen. I, for the first time, started to have dreams about him. In one particular dream, I saw him holding a baby that appeared to be six months old. He held her close and kissed her softly. Then the scene switched to me lying in bed cuddling with the baby. I watch him climb into the bed behind us and hold the both of us. I woke up puzzled. Later that day, God revealed to me the child we held was actually the daughter we would share. I wasn't too happy with the revelation. I was over little girls. I had already had two of them. But because I loved God and was obedient to Him, I said "okay God."

After that dream, I saw more visions and even started to feel him. I was blown away by what was happening. I had never felt a man's spirit besides in prayer when I prayed for my husband. Now, I started feeling tired, uneasy and confused on several occasions. When I felt these feelings, I asked God who had I been carrying because I was used to God placing different people in my spirit from time to time. So, when this happened, I knew He would tell me who I had picked up in the spirit realm. He told me each time that it was him. I would text or call him and ask him how he had felt. Initially, he would downplay his feelings. He would claim he felt okay. I knew he was trying not to complain. So, I would tell him exactly how he felt and why I knew how he really felt. At first, he was shocked because he had never experienced that before.

As time went on, we realized we started to carry each other in our spirits. There had been many occasion when he would also feel me. One day, after starting another 30 days fast, I had been feeling fire in my belly. The feeling wasn't painful at all. It was like I had been ignited in the spirit realm. Every step I took that day felt as though I was walking on new ground. It was amazing. I had never felt like that before that day. Well, as I sat working, I received a phone call from him. He stated, "I feel fire coming from your belly." *Oh my God*! That was all I could say. I was completely shocked and amazed at what was happening. He and I had been connected in the spirit realm.

Our connection went beyond just feelings. When we prayed together, we felt the power of God like we had never felt Him before. We literally felt explosions in the spirit realm. As we prayed for those who were a part of his ministry, I would see visions of them. I felt different symptoms from their ailments. I saw some of them surrendering their lives to Christ during the upcoming fast they would go on. I saw the Holy Spirit filling some in their homes. I felt them to the point that I started to carry them as well.

Covering him and his ministry resulted in me experiencing spiritual labor. One night, out of the blue, I started to have severe back pains. I initially thought I had slept incorrectly the night before. But as the day went on, the pain didn't subside; it increased. And as the days went by, I started experiencing other pregnancy symptoms. There was no way I had been pregnant in the natural. I hadn't had any physical contact with a man. So, pregnancy in the natural was impossible. But I walked around feeling as though my ankles were swollen. I had sciatica.

To ease the pain, I took pain medication which only took the edge off the pain. I was confused and worried about what I was experiencing.

After about four days of the pain, I went into deep prayer. I knew God would tell me what was going on. He revealed I had been experiencing spiritual labor; I was shocked. Before that moment, I never knew spiritual labor existed. That night, I thought about the symptoms I experienced carrying my daughters. All of the symptoms I had been experiencing were consistent. The only difference between then and now was the back pain.

After seven days of the excruciating pain, I started to feel better. I woke up that Thursday feeling lighter. I felt faint pain that was almost unnoticeable. There was no physical baby, but I did notice some difference. When I prayed that day and every day after then, I went to a deeper place. Also, when I would speak or prophesy after that day, there was a raspy sound that could be heard in my voice.

Aside from the many great spiritual things I felt from our connection, I experienced a lot of warfare. Some nights, while I slept, my mind would literally become flooded with a lot of negative thoughts whenever he and I did not pray together. There had been nights I woke up to my heart that ached as it felt as though it was on fire. I would cry and go into prayer until the feeling left my body. Afterwards, I would fall fast to sleep, only to wake up with more seeds of these negative thoughts. I consistently started to think I was not good enough and would never be good enough. I began to feel the spirit of loneliness weigh on me heavily, and I began to feel physical pain in my body. I knew these changes occurred because I had become connected to him. Even though I wanted them to stop and I desired to turn my back on the connection, I couldn't. I HAD to stay there in obedience to God.

Even though I became weak in my body and I continued to battle mental warfare, I remained committed to the process. I decided that I wasn't going to walk away from whatever the Lord was doing through our connection unless He told me to. I trusted God during this time and relied on Him for the strength I needed to get through.

Aside from being strengthened directly from God, I received strength from the men and women who were sent by God. He literally sent several prophets from different regions of the U.S. to confirm the dreams, visions, and utterances He had given us. I was completely blown away. I was astonished that God cared so much about the connection that was forming. At that time, I couldn't understand exactly why, but as time went on, the reason became clear.

The process of waiting started to take its toll on us. One afternoon, I completely fell apart and started to cry uncontrollably as we were on FaceTime. After listening to me talk, he revealed things had been difficult for him as well. After telling me he also was suffering emotionally, he stated "I can talk to my wife. I can see you. But I can't touch you." After he uttered those words, we both cried together. At that moment, no matter how much we wanted to remain strong, we *couldn't*.

God had told us both, as well as those sent, that we were husband and wife. However, the Lord specially told him we had to take things really slow. The Lord wanted us to become best of friends first. I understood the reason behind the instruction. I had always prayed to be best friends with my husband. I wanted to make sure I was completely comfortable with whoever I was to marry. I completely trusted God's judgment and wasn't going to move without Him telling me to.

Although he knew the instruction God had given, he didn't want to wait for God's timing. He desired to speed things up. Initially, he agreed with us having an actual ceremony. However, as he became more impatient, we began to disagree. Our disagreements didn't stop there. He started to put pressure on me to decide where I wanted to work. I was stunned. God had given us a specific instruction and had not changed His mind. God had not told me to look for employment. God had not changed the type of ceremony he showed me. I was not willing to step outside of the will of God. I continued to refuse as he requested.

As I refused to comply with his request, he continued to provide pressure. He requested that I research the cost of taking the bar exam in Florida. I became annoyed but still stood my ground. I reminded him the importance of remaining patient. I jogged his memory that it was imperative that we build a close relationship as God instructed first! I also told him I refused to move outside of God's perfect timing.

Although I voiced my concerns and stood my ground; he remained adamant. I recall receiving a phone call one day as I drove from work. He told me he had looked up the exam dates and fees. I was shocked. He had become so persistent. At that moment, I knew there would be tension between the two of us. Even though he stated he would help pay for the exam, I was still resistant. I had already decided come hell or high water, I was being obedient. I wasn't moving unless the Lord instructed me to move.

As time went on, he continued to apply pressure until it abruptly stopped. Before the pressure ceased, we discussed whether or not I would be renewing my lease that upcoming August. He felt as though I shouldn't renew my lease because he was sure I would be moving before the year was out to be with him. On the other hand, I was certain I wouldn't be moving before the year was out. God had told the both of us we wouldn't get married until 2018. It was still summer of 2017 at this point. After I reminded him of this, he explained that he needed his covering and couldn't wait too much longer. He expressed his firm belief that he couldn't keep going place to place preaching without his wife being there. I understood his frustration. But the fact remained, I wasn't moving outside of God's perfect timing. God had not changed His mind. Therefore, I wasn't changing mine.

Shortly after this conversation, I felt him spiritually disconnected from me. I literally felt as though a part of me had been missing. It didn't happen gradually; it happened instantly. I could no longer feel how he felt. I felt as though a piece of me was now missing and I did not like it.

The disconnection I felt spiritually manifested in the natural. The first area of manifestation was us praying separately instead of together. The next thing I noticed was there came a decrease in text messages and phone calls. After a few days of experiencing these changes, I voiced my concerns to him. Instead of admitting there had been a change, he dismissed my concerns and stated everything was okay. He blamed the lack of praying together and the decrease of communication as being due to his ministry keeping him busy. I knew deep down inside it wasn't the entire truth. I knew that there was more to it because I felt it in every area of my being.

As the days passed by, things became even worse between us. Things finally got to the point that he stopped communicating with me as he had previously. Instead of calls and text messages throughout the day, he would call 10 minutes in the morning and 10 minutes before he went to bed. I was hurt. I was livid, and I didn't want any part of the situation. I went to God in prayer and asked for permission to walk away from the connection. It was not what I wanted for my life. I couldn't see how the Lord was working in the situation. Instead of permitting me to walk away, the Lord instructed me to stay right there. He told me to continue to pray.

With each instruction, I became upset with my Creator. I couldn't understand why He would require me to stay connected to someone who obviously didn't want to be connected to me any longer. I couldn't fathom why He wouldn't grant me my desire to disconnect. I had been faithful and upright before Him. I had been obedient as much as I knew how. I just couldn't understand why He would allow me to go through what I was passing through.

During this time, the Lord continued to send His servants to deliver messages. By this time, I was tired of it. I wasn't hearing what I wanted to hear. I wasn't feeling the situation any longer. I wanted out, not another prophetic utterance telling me to hold on. However, I knew that I couldn't disregard what the Lord was saying. Deep down, I knew I needed to hear from Him as much as possible. So I listened to those He sent.

One person, in particular, had been given a prophetic dream. In that dream, he called her and told her: "Sis, I ended it." About a month after my sister-in-Christ had been given that dream, things went to the point of no return. Before the turn, the Lord had required that he and I go on 40 days fast together. The purpose of the fast was for our marriage. I really did not want to do the fast because we were barely talking. I did not want *him* to be my husband. Although I felt this way, I fasted as instructed. I knew that he did not want to fast because of the many complaints he had. Yet, I fasted anyways.

During the fasting period, I spent a lot of time in prayer. As a result, the warfare being launched up against me was greater than it had ever been in my life. It caused a greater desire to be released from the connection. I kept going before God pointing to all of the reasons I should be released from the connection. I even told God that the connection did not line up with the promises He made to me concerning the man I would marry. After I was done complaining, the Lord continued to instruct me to stay connected. He told me to continue to pray without ceasing. So I did.

The more I prayed, the more attacks were launched against my mind and body. I became really sick. At one point, I got pink eye in both of my eyes. My throat was swollen and in a lot of pain. When it became unbearable, I went to the doctors in hopes of receiving relief but was disappointed. Aside from prescribing me the medicine for my eyes, the doctor couldn't find anything medically wrong with my throat. I was appealed. I knew there had been something wrong!

At night, I struggled the most. I couldn't breathe. My eyes drained all night long. I recall waking up praying and crying as I gasped for air and wiped my eyes. Instead of giving me relief, the Lord continued to tell me to cover him in prayer. I cried even more. I was upset, yet I obeyed Him.

I continued to walk in obedience because there was no alternative. God was my king! He was my Lord! I was submitted to His will and not my own no matter what occurred.

Walking in obedience to God caused me to have many nights where my sleep was interrupted. The Lord would abruptly wake me up with visions of his face. The Lord would request for me to pray for him. I even saw two visions of things to come. Even though I did not want to pray for him, I obeyed. I didn't understand what was going on.

But I continued to pray. I had other people pray with me because there had been times I was too weak to pray.

I prayed and believed that God's will would prevail. One of the last conversations was the most heartbreaking conversations I had ever had. He told me he needed to take time to himself. He stated he needed to heal from his past. I understood completely. I didn't want to add to the pressure in his life. I wasn't trying to rush anything at all. I didn't want to uproot my daughters and move before it was time. There had been things I needed to complete in my singleness.

Though I had no desire to rush, I was still hurt. Not because he wanted to take time but because God sent me a man that was still broken. I had prayed for a man that would have already been processed; someone who knew what he wanted. Not a man that was still trying to figure out whether he wanted to obey God and His perfect timing.

During prayer, God revealed some things about what he had been secretly doing. I was upset and appalled because he had been conversing with other women though he acted as if he was extremely busy. Instead of being quiet about what I knew, I texted him. In the text, I told him everything the Lord had said to me to tell him. The messages struck a nerve with him. As a result of me sending him the messages, there had been no communication between us for several days. When we finally communicated, he sent me text messages explaining that he didn't believe I was the one for him. He further stated he felt as though I reminded him of his ex-wives. I was a reminder of his past. I was stunned and hurt. All I could think was *"God, what did you get me into?!?"* Even though I was hurt, I reassured him that I wasn't like them. I reiterated the fact that I truly wanted the best for him. After a few moments of no response, he responded: *"God, repair me because I'm tired of being damaged goods."*

I was shocked. I didn't know how to respond to his transparency. After gathering my own emotions, I responded: "I see so much in you." His only response was "I need time to pray and be with God." Even though I wanted to console him, I told him "okay."

We didn't communicate for five long days. During that time, I continued to pray that the Lord's will would prevail. On June 29, 2017, I received a text message from him. It read: "*Hello, we will not have to communicate anymore from this day forward. I'm not going to waste your time and drag things along when I'm not feeling this relationship. You're a great person but just not for me. It goes past the distance. But we don't have a lot of things in common naturally. I apologize for all the inconvenience that this has caused you. I will not contact you via phone or messenger at all. I hope and pray God sends the right one your way. I don't hate or dislike you but I know this between me and you will not work. I hope the best for you and the ministry you have, Roszien. Please, do not try to call me because I will not answer.*"

As I read each word with my mouth opened wide, I was stunned. I had never received a breakup text message before. I had never felt as disrespected like I had in that very moment. I wanted to say so many things. I wanted to tell him how I was only there because God had told me to be there. I desired to inform him how much I despised him. Every word I typed, the Holy Spirit told me to erase it. I would delete the words, only to start over again and again until I caught a hold of myself.

When I finally responded, I asked him if he was really ignoring God. I told him that I was praying for him. I informed him what he had written was not a reflection of God's will but his own will. He simply replied: "*It's nothing to discuss! You will find later on that this is the will of God that we part ways.*" After telling him it isn't, I left things as they had been.

After sending the last message, I sat still. I was stunned. But I felt the feeling of being released. It's as if after being held captive, the rejection released me. Immediately, I sent the message to my sister-in-Christ who had the dream about us. She called me almost instantly, but I couldn't talk. I called her back a few minutes later. She explained to me she had more to tell me about what she had previously dreamt. She explained she hadn't told either one of us the entire dream because she had not been permitted to by God. When she had the dream, her only assignment was to pray that it would not come to pass.

As she spoke, my anger with God turned into joy and gratitude. She told me immediately after the scene where he told her he ended it; she saw me traveling the world. She saw my business was doing well. She described how I had been smiling from ear to ear in each scene. And that I was with another man.

Instantly, I was relieved. She explained that though God's will was for us to marry, we still can reject His will for our life as he had done. And as a result of refusing God's will, he would have to deal with the consequences. At that moment, I was no longer upset because God would still honor His promise.

The days following the rejection was bittersweet. Though I no longer had to deal with someone who didn't want me, I still was hurt. I was grateful but still hurt. I couldn't understand why God would allow me to go through what I had gone through. I stayed in prayer asking God why. I needed to know so that I would be able to move forward. I knew deep down the rejection was in God's plan, but I still wanted to know why.

After I spent days crying and seeking the Lord for an answer, He answered. He allowed me to go through what I had gone through because He knew that I would tell others my testimony. He knew that going through and surviving the rejection would cause me to minister from a place where others wouldn't be able to minister from. I would minister from a place where others were too afraid to be transparent and minister.

Even though the pain had been unbearable, I was grateful the Lord chose me to go through it. He had handpicked me because He knew I was strong enough. He knew I would not turn away from Him but would turn to Him. He knew that I would obey even though I couldn't see the other side. He knew He could trust me.

After the rejection, the Lord kept me on an assignment. I had to continue to cover him in prayer. During that time, the Lord showed me different dreams and visions. In one vision, he had gotten engaged. Instead of being enraged or hurt, I continued to be obedient and pray as the Lord led me.

A few days after seeing the vision of the engagement, it was confirmed that he was in fact in a relationship. From the appearance of things, they did have plans of getting married. At that time, it had only been two weeks since he had rejected me. At that moment, I realized I had felt the spiritual disconnection because he had connected with another woman. I wasn't upset. I wasn't frustrated. I didn't hate him. I was grateful that, though I did experience some pain, I wouldn't be subjected to more pain from him.

Less than three months after rejecting me, he got married. I wasn't surprised. I was happy for the two of them. For the next several months I concentrated on moving forward and allowing the Lord to completely heal me.

Several months after experiencing the rejection, he reached out to me. I was utterly shocked and surprised. He apologized for everything he had said to me. He also told me he was angry at me for the things I said to him. That afternoon, I took ownership and apologized to him as well. I told him I had forgiven him and was happy for him and his beautiful wife. It was in that moment that I realized I had finally been healed from the rejection I had experienced. God had completely set me free!

Ultimately, this interaction led to me understanding the deeper meaning of Proverbs 16:7 *"When a man's ways please the LORD, he makes even his enemies to be at peace with him."* He had reached out to apologize to me only because the Lord laid it on his heart to do so! Had I not done as the Lord instructed me to do after being rejected by him, I would not have gotten the apology or the closure I needed.

As a result of the closure, I continued to move on in anticipation of the arrival of my husband. I knew though things didn't work out with him, God had someone special just for me. I knew that because I had endured and was obedient, the Lord would blow my mind. I knew that the next man would be everything I wanted, needed, and would be who God wanted for me and my daughters. I knew that though I had been rejected, the Lord had another. . .

PART II: SELF-REFLECTION

INTRODUCTION

Now that you've read about my journey during my wait season, it's time to reflect on your own. Although you may not be waiting on God to fulfill what He promised me, you're waiting for the manifestation of something from God. My prayer is that as you read this section, you will find clarity, that you will be provided with insight, and that you will make adjustments so that you will not cause your wait season to be longer than necessary. God bless you!

WAITING

Often, when we want something, we want it! Society has conditioned us to believe that everything should happen in an instant. When the reality is that this is far from the truth. One of the biggest things we must learn as believers is to wait on the Lord. Waiting on the Lord for anything isn't easy by any means. Not only does waiting take a tremendous amount of patience, but it takes a lot of practice. The good news is that with practice and a whole lot of dedication, waiting on God becomes easier over time.

Now that we've gotten that out of the way, let's take a quick look at king David and his process. After David was anointed king by Samuel, he didn't go immediately to the throne. Rather, he returned to the field to work. It wasn't until about twenty years later that David took his position as king.

During the time in-between being anointed as king and becoming king, David was processed by the Lord. During David's wait, the Lord revealed David's strengths and weakness to him. During David's process, the Lord showed David how to not only war in the flesh but also in the Spirit. During David's wait, he was abandoned by the ones whom he thought loved him and had to run for his life. As horrible as these encounters were, they taught David the skills he would need to be the king God desired for him to be.

No matter what you have to face during your wait season, it will prepare you for the promise. Don't put time limits on the Lord during your process because every year, day, and second is necessary.

REFLECTION QUESTIONS:
1. What promise(s) are you waiting for?

_____

_____

_____
_____
_____
_____

2. Do you believe the promise will come to pass?

_____
_____
_____
_____
_____
_____
_____
_____

3. How have you been waiting? (i.e., are you refusing to follow God's instructions? Or are you following every instruction).

_____
_____
_____
_____
_____

Prayer: Father, give us the strength to not only wait on you, but to wait in you! In the name of Jesus, Amen.

OBEDIENCE

When the Lord makes a promise to us, He is obligated to bring it to pass. 2 Corinthian 1:20 (KJV) even tell us *"For all the promises of God in him are yea, and in him Amen, unto the glory of God by us."* Amazing Right?!? It's only astonishing when we walk in complete obedience as discussed earlier.

In Genesis 17, the Lord made specific promises to Abraham and his descendants. The Lord promised to give Abraham more descendants than he could count (Genesis 17:2). The Lord also promised that Abraham's descendants would become great nations and some would become kings (Genesis 17:6). After making these promises, the Lord required Abraham and all those in his family to obey Him (Genesis 17:9). Further, as a sign that Abraham was keeping His promise to obey, Abraham was required by God to circumcise every male in his family, slaves included. Immediately after hearing the promises and what was required, Abraham *obeyed* God by performing the circumcisions.

REFLECTION QUESTIONS:
1. What instruction(s) has the Lord given to you?

_____

_____

_____

_____

_____

_____

_____

2. Have you followed the instruction(s)?

_____
_____
_____
_____
_____
_____
_____

3. If you haven't, why do you think this is so?

_____
_____
_____
_____
_____
_____
_____

4. What are some things you need to change so that you'll walk in obedience and complete every instruction?

_____
_____
_____
_____
_____
_____
_____

Prayer: Lord, help us to obey you always! In the name of Jesus, Amen.

TRUST

If you're having an issue trusting God to bring to pass the promise, don't feel bad. We all go through it at one point or another. My past momentary inability to trust God had nothing to do with Him, and *EVERYTHING* to do with me! In those moments, I had to reflect on the many situations where God did exactly what He said He would do.

Aside from reflecting on the situations where God did as promised for me, I like to reflect on the story of Samson. Before Samson's birth, an angel of the Lord appeared to Samson's mother, who had been barren, and told her she would conceive. Samson's mother was told that he would have to be dedicated as a Nazarite from birth. At this time, this was unheard because a male became a Nazarite after dedicating himself. Nevertheless, immediately after hearing this, she went and told her husband. After hearing what the angel of the Lord had said, Samson's father prayed to God for the angel to reappear to give them more instructions. The angel reappeared to them as requested and provided the parents with all the necessary directives.

Samson's parents did as the angel instructed because they trusted God. As a result of them following the instructions, they conceived Samson. Ultimately, because of their trust and obedience, God fulfilled His promise to them.

No matter how impossible the promise seems, you MUST TRUST GOD!

REFLECTION QUESTIONS:

1. Do you truly trust God will bring the promise to pass?

   _____

   _____

2. If you are having trouble trusting God, why do you think this is so?

   _____

   _____

   _____

   _____

   _____

   _____

3. What steps can YOU take to make sure you will continue to trust God to bring the promise to pass?

   _____

   _____

   _____

   _____

   _____

   _____

   _____

Prayer: Father, help us to trust you more than we trust ourselves. And when we cannot trust You, bring to our memory the past situations where You did as You said. In the precious name of Jesus, Amen.

PURPOSE

Often, we make plans for our own lives without consulting God! We neglect to ask whether our plans line up with His will. And when our plans and His plans finally clash, we become upset and frustrated and blame God for OUR mess. We do this all while neglecting to take responsibility for and refusing to let go of our purpose in pursuit of God's purpose.

The Book of Acts depicts a great example of what one should do when there is a clash between our purpose for our lives and God's purpose for us. In Acts 9, Saul went to the high priest to get them to approve him going to the synagogues in Damascus. He desired to bring Christ's disciples from Damascus to Jerusalem bound (Acts 9:1-2). Saul, after receiving the letters he sought from the high priest, journeyed to Damascus. While traveling on the road to Damascus, Saul had a life-changing encounter with the Lord.

Before the moment of Saul encountering the Lord, Saul's purpose had been to persecute Christians. He had done so much persecution and throwing Christians in jail that he was well known for it. However, instead of fighting with the Lord and refusing to submit, Saul realized he had no choice. As a result of Saul abandoning his purpose and will for his life for God's will, the Lord changed his name to Paul. Afterward, God used him as a chosen vessel to bear His name before the Gentiles, kings, and children of Israel (Acts 9:15).

The Lord has also chosen many of you reading this sentence to bear His name before man. You may be wondering why it feel as though there has been a sudden detour in your life. At one point, things seemed as though they were falling into place. Then *suddenly*, everything turned into chaos. Or you may feel as though you're now having difficulties seeing beyond where you're at. If this is you, HOLD ON!

Instead of giving up or turning back, surrender your purpose and will to God as Paul did and watch things get better.

REFLECTION QUESTIONS:

1. Have you found your purpose? If so, what is it?

_____

_____

_____

_____

_____

_____

2. If you've found your purpose, have you consulted with God?

_____

_____

3. If you haven't found your purpose, have you prayed to God for direction?

_____

_____

_____

_____

_____

_____

_____

Prayer: Father, as we seek your face and get closer to you like never before, show us who you created us to be. Lord, remove any fear that may rise up when we consider the cost of walking in purpose and our own shortcomings. Help us, Father, to remember that we can do all things through Christ. In the mighty name of Jesus, Amen.

PERSECUTION AND PURPOSE

When you are pursuing your God-given purpose, everyone will not be for you. In fact, some of the people whom you expected to be for you will be against you the most! Don't believe me? Let's take a look at Paul. As stated previously, Paul surrendered to the Lord's purpose for his life and went around Damascus preaching. Paul preached Christ to the point others were amazed while others sought to kill him (Acts 9:20-24). As a result, the disciples in Damascus snuck Paul out of Damascus at night (Acts 9:25).

After Paul escaped those who wanted to kill him in Damascus, he went to Jerusalem in hopes of joining the disciples there. Unfortunately for Paul, the disciples there were afraid of him and did not believe that he was truly a disciple (Acts 9:26). Fortunately for Paul, there was one, Barnabas, who took him to the apostles and spoke up on his behalf (Acts 9:27-31).

Despite the fact that some disciples, as well as others, did not accept Paul while walking in his purpose, Paul continued. Paul did not shut his mouth. Paul did not abort the mission he was on. Paul accepted that the Lord had chosen him as a vessel to preach. And Paul walked in it unapologetically.

Paul is a great example for us all. We must understand, despite the adversity, we must press forward. We must not get sidetracked by others. We must continue to lay down our will and purpose for our lives and pick up the will and purpose the Lord has set before us.

REFLECTION QUESTIONS:

1. Was there ever a time when you experienced persecution while walking in purpose?

   _____

   _____

2. Did the persecution cause you to stop or take a step backward? If so, why?

   _____

   _____

   _____

   _____

   _____

   _____

3. If you have been persecuted, why do you think this was so?

   _____

   _____

   _____

   _____

   _____

   _____

Prayer: Abba, give us the boldness Jesus had when persecuted. Help us oh LORD to understand that persecution is a part of the fulfillment of our purpose. Father, help us to stand still and see Your sweet salvation. In the name of Jesus, Amen.

THE OPINIONS OF OTHERS

There are times when the opinions of others are helpful. However, there are also times when the opinions of others are not so beneficial. We must be cautious not to put other people's opinions before obeying the Lord.

In Numbers 13-14, the children of Israel allowed the opinions of others to deter them from obeying the Lord. During that time, the Lord instructed Moses to send 12 men to the land of Canaan, which was the land He had promised them. As instructed by the Lord, Moses sent 12 leaders of the children of Israel with specific instructions. Moses instructed them to look at the land, to see what it was, and to report what type of people dwelt therein. Moses wanted to know whether the men were strong, weak, few, or many. Lastly, Moses instructed the 12 to bring back the fruit of the land.

After searching the land for 40 days, the men returned with a cluster of grapes and to report what they had seen. They informed Moses, Aaron, and those in the congregation that the land had flowed with milk and honey and had fruit as well. They also reported that the inhabitants of the land were strong; the cities were walled and very great. Caleb, one of the 12, then told Moses and the people they should go up and possess it because he knew they would be able to overcome its inhabitants. The other men, with the exception of Joshua, disagreed with Caleb. Instead of siding with Caleb and Joshua, the children of Israel murmured and complained. They ultimately decided they would return to Egypt.

As a result of the children of Israel listening to the opinions of the ten other men, the Lord's anger was provoked against them. The Lord decided the children of Israel, with the exception of Caleb and Joshua, would be cursed and would not enter the Promised Land. He also decided that their children would be cursed as well for 40 years. This all occurred because the children of Israel listened to the wrong opinions.

REFLECTION QUESTIONS:

1. Whose opinion do you hold close to your heart?

_____

_____

_____

2. Do you value their opinion(s) more than the Lord's?

_____

_____

3. Do they have great visions of their own? Or are they visionless?

_____

_____

4. Have they surrendered their will to the Lord/would you consider them to be godly counsel?

_____

_____

Prayer: Lord, help us to block out the opinion and voices of others. Help us, Lord, to follow your voice more than the voice of others. In the name of Jesus, Amen.

PREPARING FOR THE PROMISE

Once the Lord makes a promise to us, we sometimes make the mistake of standing still. Instead of standing still, we should prepare. Preparing for the very thing God promised prevent derailment, being sidetracked, or even abandonment.

In Genesis 6, Noah sent the time preparing as he waited for the manifestation of the flood. During that time, the Lord looked upon the face of the earth and became grieved at what He saw. His creation had been involved in so much wickedness. As a result, the Lord decided to destroy man, beast, the creeping things, and even the fowls of the air.

Even though this was the case, Noah found grace in the eyes of the Lord. As a result, the Lord told Noah what he was going to do. God instructed Noah to build an ark according to His specifications to save Noah, his family, and two of every living male and female creature (Genesis 6:18-22). Noah did as God instructed.

Though it is really unclear how long Noah waited for the manifestation, he continued to prepare as he waited (*side note: many rely on Genesis 6:3 to conclude that Noah worked 120 years until the flood came*). As a result of Noah's preparation, the ark was ready when the flood came. And Noah, his family, and a male and female of every species were saved as promised.

REFLECTION QUESTIONS:
1. Are you preparing for that which God promised you? If so, how

   are you preparing?

_____

_____

_____

_____

_____

_____

_____

2. If you have not started to prepare, what are some things you can start doing NOW?

_____

_____

_____

_____

_____

_____

_____

_____

_____

_____

3. What are some negative consequences if you fail to prepare for that which you are waiting for?

_____

_____

_____

_____

_____

_____

4. What are some positive consequences of preparation?

_____

_____

_____

_____

_____

_____

_____

Prayer: Father, give us the tenacity to prepare as we wait on You to fulfill what you've promised us. Help us to stay the course no matter what opposition we may face. Help us to have the commitment and determination like Noah. In the name of Jesus, Amen.

"The wait is always worth it when you're busy working."

ACKNOWLEDGMENT

First and foremost, I thank my Lord and Savior Jesus Christ for counting me worthy enough to be chosen and processed. I thank my mother, Esther Chism, for always pushing me to be great and for planting the seed of belief within me. I thank my daughters, Aaliyah and Myah, for consistently keeping me on my toes.

I thank my sisters, Donnika and Kamra, for always being there for me during my many melt downs; for always encouraging me to press forward; and for always being genuine and loving. There is absolutely no way I could get through life without them.

I thank my closest friend, sister in Christ, graphic designer, and book cover designer, Colbie Johnson; for always providing me with godly counsel; for assisting me in bringing my God-given visions to fruition; for always being willing to tell me when I'm wrong; and for hyping me up when I start to doubt myself. You my friend are one of the most important persons in my life.

I thank my sister in Christ Prophetess Nicole Hinton for her sincerity, for her wisdom and godly counsel, for always being one of my Simons, for being in tune with me spiritually, for all the heart emoji text messages sent, and for always understanding when it's "Christmas."

I thank my beloved humble and devoted sister in Christ, Minister Angela Crudupt, for being a willing vessel. I am grateful that she was the person who was most instrumental in pushing me to finish this book after I had put it down for months. Angela is the person God consistently uses to remind me that I am anointed to suffer for Christ.

And lastly, I thank my many spiritual mid-wives, known and unknown, for praying me through my hardest moments.

ABOUT THE AUTHOR

Roszien Kay Lewis is a devoted daughter of Jesus Christ. Her primary goal is to advance God's kingdom by encouraging, inspiring, uplifting, and advocating for others. To further this goal Roszien co-founded *My Sister's Keeper- Save Our Souls*, an organization that encourages women to live lives that are Holy and acceptable to Christ; as well as Roszien Kay LLC.

Roszien not only owns Confessions Publishing, but she authored *Confessions of An Overcomer: From Tragedy to Triumph* (Confessions Publishing, 2017). Aside from being a writer, Roszien is a Jurist Doctor who just happens to be a motivational speaker. Through her motivational speaking company, she travels around encouraging others to believe in themselves no matter what!

Additionally, Roszien remains a dedicated mother. She has two beautiful outgoing daughters, Aaliyah and Myah. Roszien and her daughters reside in Lancaster, California.

TITLES BY ROSZIEN KAY LEWIS

Confessions of An Overcomer: From Tragedy to Triumph
Confessions of An Overcomer: The Truth About the Wait

Follow Roszien on Facebook @roszienkaylewis
@confessionsofanovercomerco
On Instagram @roszienkaylewis
On YouTube @Roszien K Lewis
Email: roszien@gmail.com

www.ingramcontent.com/pod-product-compliance
Lightning Source LLC
Chambersburg PA
CBHW060950040426
42445CB00011B/1091